Arcangelo
CORELLI

(1653 – 1713)

Sonata for Violin and Basso continuo, Op. 5 No. 9
A Major / La majeur / A-Dur

Edited by
Albrecht Winter

DOWANI International

Preface

Albrecht Winter, professor of violin and music didactics at the Musikhochschule Cologne/Wuppertal and specialist in early music on modern instruments has performed this sonata for violin and basso continuo op. 5 No. 9 in A Major by Arcangelo Corelli, and has arranged the violin part. Corelli's sonatas were first published in 1700 in Rome. Further editions were published in Bologne, London and Amsterdam in the same year, and in Paris eight years later. The sonatas quickly came to enjoy international acclaim, which explains the unusually numerous publications, new editions and adaptations. Amongst others, these include several versions of the first six sonatas, all with differing ornamentation; one of which was arguably penned by the composer himself. The ornamented version of the *Adagio* in our recording is stylistically based on this version. Our edition allows you to study this piece systematically and in three varying tempi with professional accompaniments.

The CD opens with the concert version of each movement (violin and basso continuo). After tuning your instrument (Track 1), the musical work can begin. Your first practice session should be at slow tempo. If your stereo system is equipped with a balance control, you can place either the violin or the harpsichord accompaniment in the foreground by adjusting the control. The violin always remains softly audible in the background as a guide. In the middle position, both instruments can be heard at the same volume. If you do not have a balance control, you can listen to the solo part on one loudspeaker and the harpsichord part on the other. After having learnt this piece at a slow tempo, you can proceed by practising the second and fourth movements at a moderate tempo, too. We have decided against offering moderate tempo versions of the first and third movements, since the originals of both are relatively slow. Now you can play the piece with accompaniment at the original tempo. At the medium and original tempos, the continuo accompaniment can be heard on both channels (without violin) in stereo quality. All of the versions were recorded live. The names of the musicians are listed on the last page of this volume; further information can be found in the Internet at www.dowani.com.

Ornamentation and slurs have been added to the first movement of this sonata. These should however be understood as one possible interpretation and are not binding. The player should rather feel encouraged to develop his or her own ideas and should try out various possibilities (trills, mordents, inverted mordents, etc.). This version of the third movement is based on the ornamented *Adagio*-movements of the earlier editions; the notes which were written out in the original should rather be seen here as a basis for improvisation. In the 18th century, playing in first position was generally preferred, taking large string crossings into account. The fingerings printed in brackets are sometimes more difficult to play, but alter the tone quality and character of the melody line.

The realisation of the basso continuo offered here is limited to one possible basic realisation of the figured bass with a few ideas on rhythm and dynamics (reduction of number of parts to two or three parts). In passages which are repeated, the realisation of the basso continuo is often deliberately offered in different variations, to demonstrate several possible interpretations. It was not possible to print out the many various possibilities offered by the harpsichord, such as a full accompaniment, ornamentation, or arpeggio accompaniment, since they are largely dependent on the technical skill and taste of the accompanist, and also have to suit the soloist's interpretation. Accompanists who are familiar with playing basso continuo will be able to play from the figured bass part.

We wish you lots of fun playing from our *DOWANI 3 Tempi Play Along* editions and hope that your musicality and diligence will enable you to play the concert version as soon as possible. Our goal is to provide the essential conditions you need for effective practicing through motivation, enjoyment and fun.

Your DOWANI Team

Avant-propos

Albrecht Winter, professeur pour violon et didactique à l'École Supérieure de Musique de Cologne/Wuppertal et spécialiste de la Musique Ancienne sur instruments modernes a enregistré la présente Sonate pour violon et basse continue op. 5 No. 9 en La majeur d'Arcangelo Corelli et réglé la partie de violon. Les sonates de Corelli on été publiées pour la première fois en 1700 à Rome. D'autres éditions suivirent encore durant la même année à Bologne, Londres et Amsterdam, ainsi que huit ans plus tard à Paris. Ces sonates furent connues dans les pays européens très rapidement, ce qui explique les très nombreuses publications, rééditions et arrangements, parmi lesquels des versions ornementées des six premières sonates. Une de celles-ci a été probablement ornementée par le compositeur lui-même. La version ornementée de l'*Adagio* dans notre enregistrement s'oriente stylistiquement à ce modèle. Notre édition vous propose d'étudier l'œuvre de manière systématique dans trois tempos différents et avec un accompagnement professionnel.

Le CD vous permettra d'entendre d'abord la version de concert de chaque mouvement (violon et basse continue). Après avoir accordé votre instrument (plage n° 1), vous pourrez commencer le travail musical. Votre premier contact avec le morceau devrait se faire à un tempo lent. Si votre chaîne hi-fi dispose d'un réglage de balance, vous pouvez l'utiliser pour mettre au premier plan soit le violon, soit l'accompagnement de clavecin. Le violon restera cependant toujours très doucement à l'arrière-plan comme point de repère. En équilibrant la balance, vous entendrez les deux instruments à volume égal. Si vous ne disposez pas de réglage de balance, vous entendrez l'instrument soliste sur un des haut-parleurs et le clavecin sur l'autre. Après avoir étudié le morceau dans le tempo lent, vous pouvez étudier les 2e et 4e mouvements aussi dans un tempo moyen. Concernant les 1er et 3e mouvements, nous avons renoncé au tempo moyen, puisque leurs tempos originaux sont déjà relativement lents. Vous pourrez ensuite jouer le tempo original. Dans ces deux tempos vous entendrez l'accompagnement de la basse continue sur les deux canaux en stéréo (sans la partie de violon). Toutes les ver-

sions ont été enregistrées en direct. Vous trouverez les noms des artistes qui ont participé aux enregistrements sur la dernière page de cette édition ; pour obtenir plus de renseignements, veuillez consulter notre site Internet : www.dowani.com.

Dans le premier mouvement de cette sonate nous avons ajouté des ornements et des liaisons qui s'entendent, cela va sans dire, comme des propositions. Il est préférable que l'interprète développe ses propres idées et explore différentes possibilités (tremblement, pincé, mordant etc.). La version du troisième mouvement s'oriente aux mouvements d'*Adagio* ornementés des premières éditions. Les notes écrites dans l'original devront être considérées plutôt en tant que base d'improvisation. Au 18e siècle on préféra de manière générale le jeu dans la première position et des changements entre cordes éloignées furent tolérés. Les doigtés indiqués entre parenthèses sont techniquement plus difficiles par endroits, ils changent, cependant, la couleur musicale et la conduite des voix.

Notre édition se borne à une réalisation basique de la basse continue, comportant quelques suggestions concernant le rythme et la dynamique (réduction du nombre des voix à deux ou trois). Dans les passages parallèles, la réalisation a souvent été variée consciemment, afin de montrer différentes possibilités. Les nombreuses possibilités de réalisation, comme le jeu à pleine main, les ornements ou encore les arpèges, ne peuvent pas être présentées dans ce cadre puisqu'elles dépendent essentiellement du savoir-faire et du goût de l'accompagnateur et doivent aussi être en corrélation avec l'interprétation du soliste. Les accompagnateurs familiers avec la basse continue peuvent directement utiliser la partie de basse chiffrée.

Nous vous souhaitons beaucoup de plaisir à faire de la musique avec la collection *DOWANI 3 Tempi Play Along* et nous espérons que votre musicalité et votre application vous amèneront aussi rapidement que possible à la version de concert. Notre but est de vous offrir les bases nécessaires pour un travail efficace par la motivation et le plaisir.

Les Éditions DOWANI

Vorwort

Albrecht Winter, Professor für Violine und Fach-didaktik an der Musikhochschule Köln/Wuppertal und Spezialist für Alte Musik auf modernen Instrumenten, hat die vorliegende Sonate für Violine und Basso continuo op. 5 Nr. 9 in A-Dur von Arcangelo Corelli eingespielt und die Violinstimme eingerichtet. Corellis Sonaten sind erstmalig im Jahr 1700 in Rom erschienen. Weitere Ausgaben wurden noch im gleichen Jahr in Bologna, London und Amsterdam sowie acht Jahre später auch in Paris veröffentlicht. Die Sonaten gelangten schnell zu internationaler Berühmtheit. Daher gibt es außergewöhnlich viele Veröffentlichungen, Neuauflagen und Bearbeitungen, darunter verschiedene verzierte Fassungen der ersten sechs Sonaten; eine davon stammt wohl vom Komponisten selbst. Die verzierte Fassung des *Adagios* auf unserer Aufnahme ist stilistisch daran orientiert. Die vorliegende Ausgabe ermöglicht es Ihnen, das Werk systematisch und in drei verschiedenen Tempi mit professioneller Begleitung zu erarbeiten.

Auf der CD können Sie zuerst die Konzertversion (Violine und Basso continuo) eines jeden Satzes anhören. Nach dem Stimmen Ihres Instrumentes (Track 1) kann die musikalische Arbeit beginnen. Ihr erster Übe-Kontakt mit dem Stück sollte im langsamen Tempo stattfinden. Wenn Ihre Stereoanlage über einen Balance-Regler verfügt, können Sie durch Drehen des Reglers entweder die Violine oder die Cembalobegleitung stufenlos in den Vordergrund blenden. Die Violine bleibt jedoch immer – wenn auch sehr leise – hörbar. In der Mittelposition erklingen beide Instrumente gleich laut. Falls Sie keinen Balance-Regler haben, hören Sie das Soloinstrument auf dem einen Lautsprecher, das Cembalo auf dem anderen. Nachdem Sie das Stück im langsamen Tempo einstudiert haben, können Sie den zweiten und vierten Satz auch im mittleren Tempo üben. Beim ersten und dritten Satz haben wir auf das mittlere Tempo verzichtet, da sie im Original schon relativ langsam sind. Anschließend können Sie sich im Originaltempo begleiten lassen. Die Basso-continuo-Begleitung erklingt im mittleren und originalen Tempo auf beiden Kanälen (ohne Violine) in Stereo-Qualität. Alle ein-

gespielten Versionen wurden live aufgenommen. Die Namen der Künstler finden Sie auf der letzten Seite dieser Ausgabe; ausführlichere Informationen können Sie im Internet unter www.dowani.com nachlesen.

Im ersten Satz dieser Sonate wurden in der Solostimme Verzierungen und Bindungen ergänzt, die jedoch nur als Möglichkeiten zu verstehen sind. Der Spieler oder die Spielerin sollte eher eigene Ideen entwickeln und verschiedene Möglichkeiten (Triller, Mordente, Praller usw.) ausprobieren. Die Fassung des dritten Satzes orientiert sich an den verzierten *Adagio*-Sätzen der frühen Drucke; die im Original geschriebenen Noten sind hier eher als Improvisationsgrundlage zu verstehen. Im 18. Jahrhundert bevorzugte man grundsätzlich das Spiel in der ersten Lage; dabei wurden auch weite Saitenwechsel toleriert. Die in Klammern gedruckten Fingersätze sind teilweise spieltechnisch komplizierter, verändern aber die musikalische Farbgebung und Stimmführung.

Die Aussetzung des Generalbasses beschränkt sich auf eine mögliche grundlegende Realisierung des bezifferten Basses mit einigen Ideen zu Rhythmus und Dynamik (Reduzierung der Stimmenanzahl auf drei oder zwei Stimmen). An Parallelstellen wurde die Aussetzung oft bewusst variiert, um mehrere Möglichkeiten aufzuzeigen. Die vielfältigen Gestaltungsmöglichkeiten am Cembalo wie vollstimmiges Spiel, Verzierungen oder Arpeggiogestaltung sind in diesem Rahmen nicht darstellbar, denn sie obliegen dem Können und musikalischen Geschmack des Begleiters und müssen mit der Interpretation des Solisten korrespondieren. Begleiter, die mit dem Generalbassspiel vertraut sind, können aus der bezifferten Bassstimme spielen.

Wir wünschen Ihnen viel Spaß beim Musizieren mit unseren *DOWANI 3 Tempi Play Along*-Ausgaben und hoffen, dass Ihre Musikalität und Ihr Fleiß Sie möglichst bald bis zur Konzertversion führen werden. Unser Ziel ist es, Ihnen durch Motivation, Freude und Spaß die notwendigen Voraussetzungen für effektives Üben zu schaffen.

Ihr DOWANI Team

Sonata

for Violin and Basso continuo, Op. 5 No. 9
A Major / La majeur / A-Dur

A. Corelli (1653 – 1713)
Continuo Realization: M. Winter

Preludio

Giga

Arcangelo
CORELLI

(1653 – 1713)

Sonata for Violin and Basso continuo, Op. 5 No. 9
A Major / La majeur / A-Dur

Violin / Violon / Violine

DOWANI International

Violin

Sonata

for Violin and Basso continuo, Op. 5 No. 9
A Major / La majeur / A-Dur

A. Corelli (1653 – 1713)
Edited by A. Winter

Preludio

© 2007 DOWANI International, 6332 Hagendorn, Switzerland

DOW 4525

Arcangelo
CORELLI

(1653 – 1713)

Sonata for Violin and Basso continuo, Op. 5 No. 9
A Major / La majeur / A-Dur

Basso continuo / Basse continue / Generalbass

DOWANI International

Basso continuo

Sonata

for Violin and Basso continuo, Op. 5 No. 9
A Major / La majeur / A-Dur

A. Corelli (1653 – 1713)

Preludio

Giga

© 2007 DOWANI International, 6332 Hagendorn, Switzerland

DOW 4525

Tempo di Gavotta

12

Adagio

Tempo di Gavotta

Allegro

14

ENGLISH

DOWANI CD:

- Track No. 1

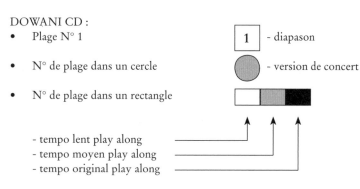

  ☐ 1 ☐ - tuning notes

- Track numbers in circles

  ⬤ - concert version

- Track numbers in squares

  ▭▭▭

  - slow Play Along Tempo
  - intermediate Play Along Tempo
  - original Play Along Tempo

- Additional tracks for longer movements or pieces

- **Concert version:** violin and basso continuo

- **Slow tempo:** channel 1: violin solo; channel 2: harpsichord accompaniment; middle position: both channels at the same volume

- **Intermediate tempo:** basso continuo only

- **Original tempo:** basso continuo only

Please note that the recorded version of the harpsichord accompaniment may differ slightly from the sheet music. This is due to the spontaneous character of live music making and the artistic freedom of the musicians. The original sheet music for the solo part is, of course, not affected.

FRANÇAIS

DOWANI CD :

- Plage N° 1

  ☐ 1 ☐ - diapason

- N° de plage dans un cercle

  ⬤ - version de concert

- N° de plage dans un rectangle

  ▭▭▭

  - tempo lent play along
  - tempo moyen play along
  - tempo original play along

- Plages supplémentaires pour mouvements ou morceaux longs

- **Version de concert :** violon et basse continue

- **Tempo lent :** 1er canal : violon solo ; 2nd canal : accompagnement de clavecin ; au milieu : les deux canaux au même volume

- **Tempo moyen :** seulement l'accompagnement de la basse continue

- **Tempo original :** seulement l'accompagnement de la basse continue

L'enregistrement de l'accompagnement de clavecin peut présenter quelques différences mineures par rapport au texte de la partition. Ceci est du à la liberté artistique des musiciens et résulte d'un jeu spontané et vivant, mais n'affecte, bien entendu, d'aucune manière la partie soliste.

DEUTSCH

DOWANI CD:

- Track Nr. 1

  ☐ 1 ☐ - Stimmtöne

- Trackangabe im Kreis

  ⬤ - Konzertversion

- Trackangabe im Rechteck

  ▭▭▭

  - langsames Play Along Tempo
  - mittleres Play Along Tempo
  - originales Play Along Tempo

- Zusätzliche Tracks bei längeren Sätzen oder Stücken

- **Konzertversion:** Violine und Basso continuo

- **Langsames Tempo:** 1. Kanal: Violine solo; 2. Kanal: Cembalobegleitung; Mitte: beide Kanäle in gleicher Lautstärke

- **Mittleres Tempo:** nur Basso continuo

- **Originaltempo:** nur Basso continuo

Die Cembalobegleitung auf der CD-Aufnahme kann gegenüber dem Notentext kleine Abweichungen aufweisen. Dies geht in der Regel auf die künstlerische Freiheit der Musiker und auf spontanes, lebendiges Musizieren zurück. Die Solostimme bleibt davon selbstverständlich unangetastet.

DOWANI - 3 Tempi Play Along is published by:
DOWANI International
A division of De Haske (International) AG
Postfach 60, CH-6332 Hagendorn
Switzerland
Phone: +41-(0)41-785 82 50 / Fax: +41-(0)41-785 82 58
Email: info@dowani.com
www.dowani.com

Recording & Digital Mastering: Wachtmann Musikproduktion, Germany
Music Notation: Notensatz Thomas Metzinger, Germany
Design: Andreas Haselwanter, Austria
Printed by: Zrinski d.d., Croatia
Made in Switzerland

Concert Version
Albrecht Winter, Violin
Mechthild Winter, Harpsichord
Isolde Winter, Baroque Cello

3 Tempi Accompaniment
Slow:
Mechthild Winter, Harpsichord

Intermediate:
Mechthild Winter, Harpsichord
Isolde Winter, Baroque Cello

Original:
Mechthild Winter, Harpsichord
Isolde Winter, Baroque Cello

© DOWANI International. All rights reserved. No part of this publication may be reproduced, stored, in a retrieval system, or transmitted in any form or by any means, electronic, mechanical, photocopying, recording, or otherwise, without the prior permission of the publisher.